PREFACE TO B

In sight-singing constant variety of treatment helps to maintain interest, and to secure this the following possible ways of using these two-part examples are suggested:

1) Each part to solfa.
2) In two parts to solfa.
3) In two parts to solfa, with expression marks.
4) Each part to laa.
5) The melody in unison (passing from stave to stave where necessary), to laa, with expression marks.
6) The descant in unison (passing from stave to stave where necessary), to laa, with expression marks.
7) In two parts to laa.
8) In two parts to laa, with expression marks, twice through.

1) The melody in unison to solfa.
2) Each part to solfa.
3) In two parts to solfa.
4) The melody in unison to laa.
5) Each part to laa.
6) In two parts to laa.
7) In two parts with expression marks, twice through.

1) Each part to solfa.
2) In two parts to solfa.
3) Each part to laa.
4) In two parts to laa.
5) The melody in unison.
6) In two parts to laa, with expression marks, twice through.

1) The melody in unison to solfa.
2) The melody in unison to solfa, with expression marks.
3) The descant in unison to solfa.
4) The descant in unison to solfa, with expression marks.
5) In two parts to solfa.
6) In two parts to laa.
7) In two parts to laa, with expression marks, twice through.

1) Each part to solfa.
2) Each part to laa.
3) In two parts to laa.
4) The melody in unison.
5) In two parts to laa, with expression marks, twice through.

1) In two parts to solfa.
2) The melody in unison to laa.
3) Each part to laa.
4) In two parts to laa.
5) In two parts to laa, with expression marks, twice through.

1) In two parts to solfa.
2) In two parts to laa.
3) The melody in unison to laa.
4) In two parts to laa, with expression marks, twice through.

Sometimes the melody only may be sung through, each part taking the section which belongs to its stave. Sometimes the descant may be treated similarly. There are many other ways of practising these examples; the teacher should not rest content with those given above.

When the parts are read separately, the other portion of the class must follow and be invited to 'spot' mistakes. Sometimes both divisions of the class should learn both lines.

Neither section of the class should be kept permanently to first or second line; one should take the upper in one example and the lower in the next, as the examples are written for equal voices. The class should point out all imitations, augmentations, diminutions, etc.

A free contrapuntal style has generally been adopted in order that the singers may cultivate independence. Except where the treatment is canonical, the melody should always be slightly more prominent than the descant; there are various degrees of f, various degrees of p, etc. The class should always beat time, or, in such cases as slow 6/8, tap each beat silently.

It has not been thought necessary to refrain from including a few familiar tunes, because the descants will provide material for sight-reading.

Note.—The Editors wish to express their indebtedness to Messrs Bela Bartok and Karol Hlawiczka for kind permission to use many fine Hungarian and Polish tunes from their collections. It may be noted that in these, as well as in other melodies, the phrasing seems unusual, but it has been dictated by the original words.

INDEX

FOLK-SONG SIGHT SINGING SERIES
BOOK VIII
SECTION I. Nos. 1-39
Major Mode

Chorale

German

2

Polish

Allegretto

Swiss

Moderato 3 + 3 + 2 + 3

Dutch

Andante Begins on lah. 3 bar rhythm.

6

8

Allegro When mastered, sing quickly, one beat in a bar.

Hungarian

German

French

Polish

Allegro 3 + 2 + 2 + 3 Note sequence. When mastered, sing more quickly, one beat in a bar.

French

Allegro moderato 4 bars answered by 6. May be taken in E♭

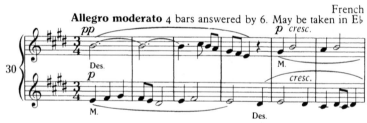

SECTION II. Nos. 40-50

Minor Mode